Forging a Strong Mother-Daughter Bond

Beyond Manipulation and Control

Leslie Vernick

New Growth Press
www.newgrowthpress.com

New Growth Press, Greensboro, NC 27404
www.newgrowthpress.com
Copyright © 2013 by Leslie Vernick

All rights reserved. No part of this publication may be reproduced, stored in a retrieval system, or transmitted in any form by any means, electronic, mechanical, photocopy, recording, or otherwise, without the prior permission of the publisher, except as provided by USA copyright law. Published 2013.

All Scripture quotations, unless otherwise indicated are from *The Holy Bible, English Standard Version*® (ESV®), copyright © 2000, 2001 by Crossway Bibles, a division of Good News Publishers. Used by permission. All rights reserved.
  Scripture quotations marked NIV are taken from the *Holy Bible*, New International Version®, NIV®. Copyright © 1973, 1978, 1984, 2011 by Biblica, Inc. Used by permission. All rights reserved worldwide.

Cover Design: Faceout books, faceout.com
Typesetting: Lisa Parnell, lparnell.com

ISBN-10: 1-939946-13-1
ISBN-13: 978-1-939946-13-3

Library of Congress Cataloging-in-Publication Data
Vernick, Leslie.
 Forging a strong mother-daughter bond : beyond manipulation and control / author Leslie Vernick.
    pages cm
 Includes bibliographical references and index.
 ISBN 978-1-939946-13-3 (alk. paper)
 1. Mothers and daughters—Religious aspects—Christianity.
2. Mothers and daughters—Psychology. I. Title.
 BV4529.18.V47 2013
 248.8'431—dc23   2013018496

Printed in China

25 24 23 22 21 20 19 18   3 4 5 6 7

Carla[1] stared at the caller ID, though she already knew who was calling. It was her mother . . . again. She wanted Carla and her family to travel home for the holidays. But Carla and her husband had decided to stay home this year, and she knew her mother would not accept her refusal without protest. Her stomach turned flip-flops as she answered the phone. Once more Carla tried to explain to her mother why she and her husband Bill thought it best to stay home this Christmas: The kids were getting older and wanted to do things over the holidays with friends. She and Bill wanted to start some of their own family traditions. Plus, it was a long drive, and they were both exhausted from work. It was no use; Carla felt like she was speaking to the wall.

"It just wouldn't be the same without you and the grandchildren here with us," Carla's mother sighed. "You just have to come home. I won't hear anymore about it." This wasn't the first time her mom cranked up the pressure to push Carla to give in. Carla remembered dreading her own wedding. All her ideas had to take a backseat to what Mom thought best—or there was a price to pay. Carla also regretted not attending the college of her choice because her mother felt it was too far from home. While she was growing up, Mom always demanded—and got—what she wanted.

Carla started feeling furious—both at herself for always giving in and at her mother for not freeing her to be her own person. But her fury was quickly masked over by guilt and anxiety. Maybe she was being selfish. She wouldn't always have her parents with her, and maybe her mother was right; she and Bill should put them first. Carla loved her mother and father and wanted to be a good daughter. She was a Christian and wanted to obey God by honoring her parents.

But did that mean she had no choices? Does being a good Christian mean she must always go along with whatever her mom wants or demands in order to honor her, keep the peace, or have a good relationship with her? Carla wanted a close relationship with her mom, but she feared that they could only be close if Carla did exactly what her mom wanted. Was there another way?

It's not just daughters who don't know how to build an honest, close relationship with their moms; moms struggle with their daughters too. Lydia loves her family and wants to make them happy. During the years her daughter Kim was growing up, Lydia gave and gave, never looking for anything in return. She thought that was God's way. Now that her daughter is grown, she's beginning to feel taken advantage of. For example, Kim accepted a full-time job, assuming Lydia would babysit her three children. Lydia didn't feel like she could say no, even though she had already told Kim how excited she was to finally have the chance to return to college. To top it off, her husband Steve and Kim both forgot her fiftieth birthday. When she mentioned how hurt she felt, they just laughed and made lame apologies.

Lydia was beginning to realize that her family wasn't as close as she had thought. She saw that the more she gave, the more Steve and Kim expected, with little concern for her. Although Lydia didn't intend this, her actions allowed her family to become more and more self-centered, self-absorbed, and selfish. Lydia didn't mean to, but by living for their approval rather than God's, she weakened her husband and daughter by not inviting them into a relationship of mutual love and care. She also contributed to their growing pattern of manipulation because she never learned how to stop it. Lydia felt resentful that her own life was continually on hold while she made sure her daughter's and husband's life flowed well.

Lydia wanted a strong mother-daughter relationship with Kim, just as Carla did with her mother. But neither was quite sure how to change the patterns that made her so afraid to say no. They wanted to love as Christ would have them to, but didn't know how to break free from their guilt, fear, and people pleasing.

Does Loving Someone Mean Never Saying "No"?

Relationships are important to God. All of the Ten Commandments address either our relationship with God or our relationship with one another (Exodus 20). Jesus summed them up when he said that the two most important ones are, "'Love the Lord your God with all your heart and with all your soul and with all your mind and with all your strength.' The second is this: 'You shall love your neighbor as yourself.' There is no commandment greater than these" (Mark 12:30–31).

But does loving someone require that we never say no? Does it mean we always put the other person's needs, wants, and feelings above our own? For a mother it can be difficult to say no to her daughter. After all, we want her to be happy and achieve her dreams even if, like Lydia, we sacrifice our own dreams. Like Carla, as a grown daughter, it's hard to disappoint our mother after all she's done for us. It seems selfish to say no when something as simple as going home for Christmas means so much to her. Yet both Carla and Lydia also felt uneasy and angry inside. They felt afraid to say no, and pressured to always give in. As we grow to understand biblical love better, we learn that sometimes it's not only appropriate to say no, but wise and right.

Manipulation is nothing new. Both mothers and daughters can struggle with feeling manipulated or with trying to manipulate others. It is one of the strategies we fallen human beings use to control other people and get our own way. Sometimes we don't recognize that we're trying to manipulate someone or that we're being manipulated. It's what we know. It's how we've learned to avoid having to deal with disappointment, disagreement, and differences. But when manipulation is a part of our relationships, it's destructive and damages the relationship God intended.

Carla desired a good relationship with her mother, as did Lydia with her daughter. But Carla responded to her mother's attempts to control her with anger and resentment. Carla felt that she couldn't be honest with her mother about her own feelings and needs because her mother regularly dismissed them as invalid or unimportant. This hurt Carla deeply. Kim's disregard for her mother also deeply hurt Lydia. She excused it when Kim was young, but now that her daughter was an adult, she saw how selfish Kim had become.

Carla's mother would be shocked and hurt to hear that her daughter was starting to resent her and pull away. This was the last thing she wanted. She, too, desired a close mother-daughter bond and didn't realize how her manipulative tactics were destroying the very thing she wanted. Kim, too, would be surprised to hear how deeply her mother was starting to resent the time and energy she spent always being available.

How to Recognize Manipulation

The following examples are the most common forms of manipulation. As you read through them, ask yourself about your relationship with your mom or your daughter. Are you more likely to be the manipulator or the person who is being manipulated? For most of us, it's a little bit of both.

1. Guilt Trips

This kind of manipulator tries to make you feel bad, shamed, or guilty for saying no, expressing your own thoughts, feelings, or needs. Carla's mother tried to make Carla feel like she was a selfish, unloving, daughter because she didn't want to come home for Christmas.

A biblical example is when Laban said Jacob had tricked him by taking his family and livestock away from Laban's compound without his knowledge. He wanted Jacob to feel guilty for leaving, despite the fact that Laban had been the one who had consistently tricked and deceived Jacob (Genesis 31:25–30).

2. Pleading and Begging

This kind of manipulator begs and repeats something over and over again, trying to wear you down. "Please? Pleeease? Pleeeeeeeeeeeeeeese?" Lydia's daughter begged Lydia to come over and babysit the children for the day so she could have a break, although Lydia did not feel well. "Mom, you know how hard I work. I just need this little break. You'll be fine."

A biblical example is when Potiphar's wife attempted to seduce Joseph, day after day, not respecting his no (Genesis 39:6–12).

3. Crying, Sulking, and Withdrawing

This is a form of threatening behavior where the underlying message is that if you don't do what I want you to, I won't be able to function or survive—or there will be a price to pay. These forms of manipulation are mostly nonverbal. Sulking, sobbing, slamming doors, and the silent treatment were the tactics Carla's mother used to control Carla's college and wedding choices. Lydia's daughter also used this tactic in order to get Lydia to agree to cosign a loan to remodel her home. Several weeks of no contact with her grandchildren were enough to scare Lydia into saying yes to her daughter's demands.

A biblical example is Samson's wife crying and accusing him of not loving her because he would not tell her the answer to the riddle he posed to the men of the city (Judges 14:16–17).

4. Misquoting You or Others

In one of their many phone conversations, Carla's mom told her, "Your brother and sister are very disappointed in you." Carla immediately e-mailed her sister and asked if it was true. Her sister responded that what she had told their mother was that she was disappointed Carla wasn't coming home. She also told Carla she admired her courage for standing up to their mother, something she found impossible to do.

A biblical example is when Satan misquoted God to Eve, telling her that she wouldn't die (Genesis 3:4), and when Satan misquoted God's Word to Jesus in his desert temptation in order to get him to do what he desired him to do (Matthew 4:5–6).

5. Bullying and Threats

This type of manipulation is usually a tactic a manipulator will use after other attempts at control have failed. It's a last-ditch effort to get you to do or not do what she desires. When Lydia worked up her courage and told her daughter she didn't want to babysit every day because she wanted to go back to college, her daughter said, "Fine. With your new schedule you'll be too busy studying to see the grandkids on weekends either."

A biblical example is found throughout the book of Nehemiah when certain individuals tried to keep Nehemiah from rebuilding the wall (see 2:19; 4:1, 5–6). The bully's message is if you don't do what I want, you'll have a heavy price to pay.

6. Name Calling, Personal Attacks, and Constant Criticism

These attacks are meant to make you feel insecure, guilty, ashamed, and stupid so that you will second-guess your decision or change your mind. In one of their phone conversations, Carla's mom told her, "I can't believe you're being so selfish and stubborn. Obviously you and Bill don't care about the family like we thought you did."

The biblical book of Nehemiah is full of examples of this type of manipulation (Nehemiah 4:1–2; 6). In the New Testament the Pharisees regularly criticized Jesus and questioned his credibility as a way of undermining him and trying to get him to stop his ministry. (See, for example, Matthew 12:24.)

7. Empty Promises

"Just come for Christmas this year. We can do things differently next year." Carla heard those empty promises throughout her wedding planning. Mom promised, "Just let me do the flowers my way, and you can pick the music." But when Carla chose music her mother didn't approve of, her mother sulked until Carla gave in. Lydia's daughter promised to make timely payments on the loan if Lydia would cosign. But it never happened. Lydia ended up having to pick up the payment because she was afraid her credit rating would be ruined if she didn't.

Satan is a master at making empty promises to deceive and mislead us into doing what he wants us to do. If you eat this fruit, you will be like God, he says (Genesis 3:4; see also Matthew 4:9).

8. Appealing to a Higher Authority

"God says you're to honor your father and mother. I don't see any honoring in your decision to stay away from us." There are legitimate times to appeal to a higher authority (God, the Scriptures, and legal authorities) in the hopes of bringing a sinner to her senses. However, when we regularly use this as a means of controlling someone, it's manipulative.

The Pharisees used this approach with Jesus, appealing to the Law of Moses to try to get him to stop what he was doing (see, for example, Matthew 12:10; 21:23).

9. Lying—by Omission or Commission

When we don't tell the whole truth or we twist information to make it look one way or another, we are lying in an attempt to control someone else. Lydia's daughter implied that they did not have enough money to pay for childcare. However, when she and her husband took the kids to Disney World and stayed at an expensive hotel for a week, Lydia felt even more resentful. Lydia was not only making payments on their loan, but she was not getting paid to watch the grandchildren.

The Bible tells of Rebekah encouraging her son Jacob to dress up as his brother in order to deceive Isaac into blessing Jacob—thinking he was Esau (Genesis 27). Another example is King Saul lying to Samuel about following the Lord's commands to influence Samuel to think he fully obeyed God (1 Samuel 15:15–17).

If you are the one who is being manipulated it's important to understand that you can't change the manipulator when you confront her directly. Like Lydia's daughter or Carla's mother did, the manipulator will just switch to another tactic and attempt to wear you down. It's tempting for Carla and Lydia to place the entire responsibility of change on Carla's mom and Lydia's daughter. However, if you are unhappy and want to change your interactions with your mother, your daughter, or anyone else who is manipulating you, the change must start with you. Carla and Lydia needed to look at what was going on in their hearts that allowed them to be manipulated.

Three Reasons We Allow Ourselves to Be Manipulated

1. Fear

Carla allowed her mother to manipulate her because she was afraid of her mom's reaction. Likewise, Lydia hated when her daughter expressed disappointment or anger toward her. In the past, when each tried to be honest, the other person's disapproval, anger, and unhappiness always caused them to cave in. When Carla stood firm on her decision regarding the holidays, she feared her mother would retaliate, sulk, and not speak to her for several months because those were her mother's usual patterns. When Lydia tried to stand firm on not babysitting her grandchildren every day, she feared her daughter would follow through on her threats, and she wouldn't be able to see the grandchildren very often.

Like Carla and Lydia, we fear that if we don't give in to the manipulator's demands, something bad might happen and it would be our fault. We worry that if we don't do what the other person wants, we will lose her love and perhaps even the relationship. These fears are possibilities with a manipulative person. Carla or Lydia may have to endure their loved one not speaking to her for a while if she doesn't give in to the other's wishes.

Moving Beyond Fear

The Bible warns us that the fear of man lays a snare (Proverbs 29:25). When we are controlled by fear, we can't love well. God tells us to anchor ourselves in his love, not in the love of another fallen human, even if that person is as close as our own mother or daughter. When we are confident of God's love for us, it empowers us to love others well without being held captive by their demands. Perfect love casts out fear (1 John 4:18). Therefore, we don't have to react negatively to the manipulator's tactics, but we respond kindly, yet firmly, with our no.

Carla wanted to know how to show love and respect to her mother without having to capitulate to her demands. To start, Carla had to mentally and emotionally accept that her mother would feel disappointed and angry with her decision not to come home. Accepting someone's disappointment with us is easier said than done. We don't like people to be angry with us. Carla wanted her mother to approve and be happy with her decisions.

It's more realistic to acknowledge that most people (even our mothers or our daughters) won't feel happy when we won't do what they want. That's not manipulative; it's human. But in a good mother-daughter relationship, we don't use our upset or negative feelings to retaliate or manipulate in order to get our own way. We understand that sometimes we don't get what we want. We accept that our daughter or mother has separate feelings and needs of her own, and we let our negative emotions go and move on for the good of our relationship.

Carla prayed and asked God for courage to be firm, yet loving, with her mother. She said, "Mom, I know sharing Christmas together means a lot to you, and I respect that. I hope my kids will come to visit me on Christmas when they get older. But this year it's just not going to work for us. We love you and will be thinking about you. We can Skype if you'd like, but I don't want to keep talking about it. We are not going to change our mind."

Carla was able to say those words and remain firm in her decision because she realized that she no longer needed her mother to approve of her decision or even be happy with it. As Carla's relationship with God deepened, she realized that she had mistakenly allowed her mother to take God's place in her life. Her mother, not God, shaped how she should think and told her what she should do. As Carla began to grasp God's perfect love for her in Christ, it freed her from having to please her mother in order to feel secure. She was already secure in God. That was enough.

When Carla gave her mother her final answer, her mother hung up on her and for the next several weeks she gave Carla the silent treatment. It was tough for Carla not to get swept back into her normal anxiety and fear about disappointing her mother, but she stayed focused on pleasing God and not on her mother. It's not that she didn't care about her mother's feelings; she did. But she learned that she could show empathy and compassion for someone else's sadness, hurt, and even anger and still not accommodate them or reverse her decision. She felt freer simply to love her mother when she didn't fear her negative reaction as much.

2. Guilt

A second reason we become an easy target for manipulators is because we feel guilty whenever we say no. Like Lydia, when we attempt to speak up or share our own feelings and needs, manipulators exploit our sensitive conscience and often tell us that we are selfish and wrong if we don't always do what they want. Manipulators define love in a skewed way. They might even say, "If you loved me, you'd do what I want." Two-year-olds use this tactic on their mother to get her to buy them something while standing in line at the grocery store. Most mothers are wise enough not to be manipulated by these tantrums. Nor do they feel guilty when they say no to their child. We know that a firm "no" to our child is the most loving thing we can do.

The same is true for other relationships. Saying no to manipulation is actually taking a stand against someone's sin. This is a good thing!

When the manipulator is our mother or an adult daughter having a tantrum, it's much harder not to get sucked into her drama. When she accuses us of being unloving and selfish because we're not giving into her demands, we're tempted to feel guilty. It's tough to stay clear-minded and firm under that kind of pressure.

Moving beyond Guilt

We know that Jesus never sinned. He was always loving, never selfish, yet he did say no and didn't always do what everyone wanted or expected him to do. Jesus took time out for friendship, rest, relaxation, and prayer (Mark 6:30–31, 46). When you feel guilty because you've said no to someone, take a moment to read Mark 1:29–39. In this passage we learn that Jesus went to Simon Peter's house for a relaxing dinner, but people brought the sick to Jesus and the whole town gathered at the door. Can you imagine the pressure Jesus felt with everyone pressing in on him to do something? That evening he healed many people, but he eventually said no more and went to sleep. Those who were left unhealed must have felt disappointed.

While it was still dark, Jesus woke up and went off by himself to pray. Peter eventually came looking for him. "Jesus, where have you been? Everyone back home is waiting for you." Jesus answered Peter saying, "I'm not going back to your house. Let's go somewhere else—to the nearby villages—so I can preach there also. That is why I have come."

Jesus knew he could not do everything everyone wanted him to do and still do what God wanted him to do. During that quiet time of prayer, Jesus asked the Father to help him discern between the good things and the best things. Just like we do, Jesus had to make some hard choices—to please God or to please others. He chose pleasing God. Jesus describes himself as always doing what his Father wanted him to do. That focus regularly cost him the disapproval and disappointment of others, including his disciples, religious leaders, and family (see Matthew 26:8; Mark 3:21–22).

If we want to break free from the trap of guilt, we must learn to distinguish the difference between true guilt and false guilt. True guilt is a God-given warning signal that we are violating his moral law. False guilt results when we or another human being judges our actions, ideas, or feelings as wrong, even if there is nothing sinful about them.

Lydia struggled because she wasn't sure if her guilty feelings were from God or because her daughter disapproved of her decision to stop watching her grandchildren full-time and return to college. Her first step was to go directly to God for clarification. We can pray and ask God to search us and know our anxious thoughts and see if there is any wicked way in us (Psalm 139:23–24). We can trust the Holy Spirit to bring to mind if there is anything we need to repent of or do differently. For example, Lydia realized that she did have a lot of resentment toward her daughter that she needed to repent of and let go of. But she also knew that letting her resentment go and forgiving her daughter didn't mean enabling her daughter's selfishness or manipulation to continue by saying yes to more babysitting.

Jesus never violated God's moral law so he was never guilty. And he refused to accept false guilt about disappointing people who expected otherwise. Jesus never equated love with being accommodating.

That brings us to the last reason we allow ourselves to be easily manipulated by others. We live for the approval of others and fear their disapproval.

3. Living for the Approval of Others

Lydia realized she was becoming more and more exhausted as she cared for others without time for herself, or God. She so feared disappointing others that she allowed them to define her purpose and her value. From her family's perspective, her sole purpose was to do for and give to them. When she failed or refused, her value diminished in their eyes.

This is not the way God calls us to live. He doesn't want us to be people-centered women, but rather God-centered women. God calls us to love others, but we will get in trouble if we love them more than we love God. God says that what we love the most will rule us and control us (2 Corinthians 5:14). When we love God first, he will show us how to love others well. When we are too nice or overly accommodating, living for people's approval rather than God's, we not only hurt ourselves, we hurt others as well.

Beyond Manipulation to God-Honoring Relationships

God shows us what our relationships should look like in the Trinity. The Father loves and glorifies the Son. The Son loves and honors the Father. Both value the work of the Holy Spirit, and the Holy Spirit reflects glory back to Jesus and the Father. God gave Jesus the freedom to decide whether to sacrifice his life, and Jesus desired to obey and submit to his Father. The three persons of the Trinity complement and honor one another.

In a similar way, God-honoring human relationships require three essential ingredients: mutuality, reciprocity, and freedom. *Mutuality* means that both people bring to the relationship certain qualities such as caring, respect, and honesty. When only one person is doing all the caring, respecting, or being honest, you can't have a close relationship even if you love that person, even if you are in the same family. The apostle Paul asked for mutuality with the Corinthian church. He said, "We have spoken freely to you, Corinthians, and opened wide our hearts to you. We are not withholding our affection from you, but you are withholding yours from us. As a fair exchange—I speak as to my children—open wide your hearts also" (2 Corinthians 6:11–13 NIV).

Reciprocity involves give and take where both people in the relationship share power and responsibility. There is not a double standard where one person does most of the taking and the other person sacrificially does most of the giving. Those types of relationships are typically more ministry than close friendships. However, even with ministry relationships we can feel taken advantage of. When we are called to give sacrificially, we are to do so in order to bring about someone's good, not to enable their sin or selfishness to flourish. The apostle Paul gave guidelines to churches on giving their resources sacrificially, but not foolishly. He wrote, "For I do not mean that others should be eased and you burdened, but that as a matter of fairness your abundance at the present time should supply their need, so that their abundance may supply your need, that there may be fairness" (2 Corinthians 8:13–14).

Lastly, a God-honoring relationship requires *freedom*. Freedom in a relationship means you are allowed to make choices, to give input, and to say no without being badgered, manipulated, and punished. Freedom empowers you to be and express the person God made you to be without fear of retaliation or rejection. God has made each of us unique and separate individuals, and he has given us the freedom to choose. In a God-honoring relationship the other person validates and appreciates our uniqueness and differences. We're not afraid to be ourselves, nor are we pressured to become something we're not. Paul regularly validated the unique contributions to his life that people made. He appreciated their gifts and strengths and did not expect people to be the same. He also spoke about different parts of the body of Christ, each with different personalities, gifts, and abilities, all vital for the whole to function (1 Corinthians 12).

All human relationships do involve some angst and struggle because, unlike the Trinity, we are sinful. However, when a conflict arises, mature people engage in conversations where they discuss, negotiate, compromise, and respect one another's differences, feelings, and desires. On the other hand, a manipulator pushes and pressures to get his or her own way by ignoring stated or implied boundaries, trying to get the other to back down or feel guilty or afraid so that they will give in.

When mutuality, reciprocity, and freedom are lacking in our relationship with someone we love, like Carla and her mother, or Lydia and her daughter, the relationship becomes difficult and sometimes destructive. It feels more like ministry or misery than close friendship.

A Courageous Risk

If you want to change a manipulative mother-daughter relationship, you will need to risk disapproval and possibly rejection in order to get there. That's why it's essential to move beyond fear, false guilt, and trying to please. You need the Spirit's help so that you can tolerate someone else's disappointment when you say no.

When a manipulator realizes that you aren't going to give in to her demands no matter what, usually one of two things will happen. Either the manipulator will begin to back down and learn to treat you with respect, or the relationship will deteriorate and possibly end for a season because the manipulator is retaliating. I'm sure you don't want your relationship with your mother or daughter to end. But consider the alternative. Do you want to be held hostage by your fear of what might happen? Your fear of being rejected? Your fear of losing the relationship? The unceasing demands on your time, your energy, and your money?

As we center ourselves on God's love and aim to please him first, we can trust him with the outcome of our relationship. We will never have a good or close mother-daughter bond when our relationship is structured around fear or guilt. When we allow ourselves to be held captive to what might happen or another person's demands, please understand that the relationship has already deteriorated. The Bible says love does not demand its own way (1 Corinthians 13:5).

Carla's mother and Lydia's daughter continued to pressure them on many things, but as Lydia and Carla practiced standing strong in Christ and refused to be manipulated, over time, Carla's mother, and Lydia's daughter grew more respectful.

What If You Are the Manipulator?

If, as you read this minibook, you realize that you also struggle with manipulating, ask yourself whether you would rather have a close, honest relationship with your mother or daughter or have your own way? One of the most important things you need to do if you want to forge a close mother-daughter relationship is tolerate pain when you don't get your way. That's one of the reasons Carla's mom kept the pressure up. She didn't know how to deal with the hurt and disappointment of Carla and her family not being there on Christmas. She didn't want to feel that sadness or anger, and therefore she continued to pressure Carla to change her mind.

Jesus reminds us that in this world we will have pain and suffering, but we can bear it when we put our hope in him. This frees us from putting all of our hope in getting everything we want or believe we need. If you desire a good relationship with your daughter or your mother, you must allow her the freedom to say no without retaliating against her when she does, or pressuring her to change her mind. A good adult mother-daughter relationship is only formed when both mother and daughter can freely make choices without fear or guilt. When one person has all the power and the other feels powerless, you end up with either compliance or rebellion, but you will never share intimacy, love, or respect together.

Even when you recognize them, the habits of manipulation are not easily changed. A good first step is to confess to your daughter or mother that you realize you have pressured and manipulated her and you want to stop. This is repentance. But a change of mind and heart also needs to grow into a change of habit. Ask your mother or daughter to speak up when she feels you are not accepting her no or are trying to pressure her to change her mind about something. When she takes that risk and does so, thank her and accept her words as God's warning bell for you to stop manipulating. As your daughter or mother sees that you take responsibility when you are manipulating and as she experiences your genuine efforts to change, she will be encouraged that she can disagree, be different, or say no to you and that you can still share a close mother-daughter bond. In fact, you will share a bond that surpasses what you had with the manipulation.

Don't forget—God wants us to have good relationships, but manipulation will never get us there. God gives us the Holy Spirit to empower us to grow and change to be better mothers and better daughters. See how centering yourself in God's love and depending on his approval rather than a person's approval can bring change and healing to you and your relationship with your mother or your daughter. Whether you are tempted to manipulate or tempted to give in to manipulation, trust God for your relationship.

Endnotes

1. Carla and Lydia are not their real names, but are composites of actual case situations I have seen over the years.